SEVEN WONDERS
OF THE
ANCIENT WORLD

Hugh Gethin

Judith Brown

GEORGIAN PRESS

Georgian Press (Jersey) Limited
8 Duhamel Place
St Helier
Jersey JE2 4TP
Channel Islands

© Hugh Gethin and Judith Brown 1994

First published by Georgian Press (Jersey) Limited 1994

ISBN 1-873630-07-7

Produced by Banson, 3 Turville Street, London E2 7HR
Cover design and map by Roger Whisker
Printed in Great Britain

Acknowledgements

The publishers are grateful to the following for permission to reproduce photographs; and to John Urling Clark who did the photo research.

The J. Allan Cash Photolibrary: pages 17, 30, 56.

The Ancient Art & Architecture Collection: pages 39, 41, and the cover photograph.

Hulton Deutsch Collection Limited: pages 12, 14, 25, 34, 35, 44, 53, 63, 65, 73.

The authors are indebted to the following publication:

The Seven Wonders of the Ancient World, edited by Peter A. Clayton & Martin J. Price (Routledge, 1988).

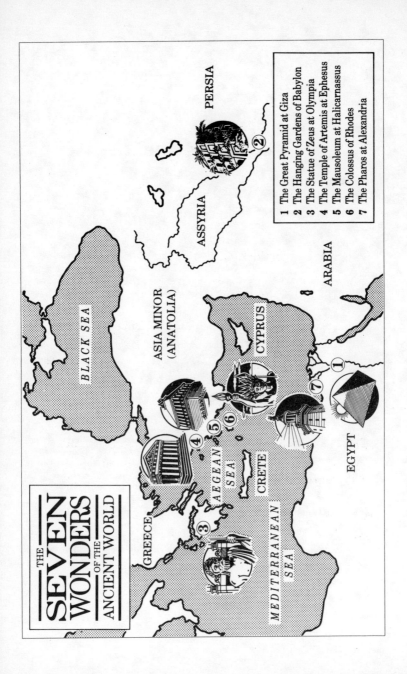

THE
SEVEN
WONDERS
OF THE
ANCIENT WORLD

BLACK SEA

ASIA MINOR
(ANATOLIA)

GREECE

AEGEAN
SEA

CRETE

MEDITERRANEAN
SEA

CYPRUS

EGYPT

ASSYRIA

PERSIA

ARABIA

1 The Great Pyramid at Giza
2 The Hanging Gardens of Babylon
3 The Statue of Zeus at Olympia
4 The Temple of Artemis at Ephesus
5 The Mausoleum at Halicarnassus
6 The Colossus of Rhodes
7 The Pharos at Alexandria

Contents

Introduction

More people than ever before now travel to see the wonders of the world. Some are natural wonders, such as mountains and volcanoes, waterfalls and canyons, and the wildlife of plains and forests. Others are famous wonders made by man, such as the Pyramids of Egypt or Mexico, the Great Wall of China, the Taj Mahal, the Parthenon, the Colosseum, Venice, Machu Picchu... The list may be long, but travellers shorten it to the things that impress them most, whether by their size, by their beauty, or by the skill that went into their making.

The habit is an old one, and goes back to the time when people were first able to travel for their own education and pleasure, instead of being forced to do so by enemies or by hunger. The Greek historian Herodotus was one of the earliest of such travellers. In the fifth century BC he went to Persia and to Egypt and visited both the city of Babylon and the Pyramids. He wrote down what he saw and what he was told, and so became one of the first travel writers. His readers were able, like Herodotus himself, to marvel at the wonderful things he described.

With the conquests of Alexander the Great in the following century and the spread of the Greek language, the number of travellers increased. And as, in turn, the Roman empire grew, travelling became easier still. There were more books, too, and there were libraries, such as the splendid ones at Alexandria in Egypt and at Pergamum in Anatolia, to keep them in. With the travellers and the books there came stories – travellers' tales like those of Herodotus – of the wonders that were seen. Comparisons were made, lists were drawn up. One of them was a list of seven made by Antipater of Sidon in the second century BC. With one exception it is the same as the list we now have of the Seven Wonders of the Ancient World.

That the number chosen was seven is not, of course, surprising. Among the numbers one to ten, seven has for a long time been special. Like the numbers three and five, no other number except one will divide into it, but unlike five, it cannot be multiplied to make ten. And so we have not only the Seven Wonders but also the Seven Stars (the Pleiades), the Seven Wise Men, the Seven Seas, the Seven Hills of Rome, the Seven Deadly Sins, and many more.

Other classical authors followed Antipater in writing of the Seven Wonders. They did not always mention all seven, and if they did, they did not always name the same ones. But it is clear that the idea of a list of Wonders gradually became accepted. When the Roman empire fell, the tradition was kept alive by some early Christian writers. Then, with the European Renaissance at the end of the fifteenth century AD, the idea of the Seven Wonders of the Ancient World was fully reborn, and the list as we know it today was finally agreed.

As we have said, our modern-day list is the same as Antipater's with one exception. Whereas his list included the Walls of Babylon, we now have instead the Pharos or Lighthouse at Alexandria. This change to the list of Wonders was made in the fourth century AD, when the lighthouse had been standing for nearly six hundred years and had become famous as the first and biggest of its kind. The other six Wonders are the Great Pyramid at Giza, the

Hanging Gardens of Babylon, the Statue of Zeus at Olympia, the Temple of Artemis at Ephesus, the Mausoleum at Halicarnassus and the Colossus of Rhodes.

When we look at the list we may ask ourselves why it is made up of these particular seven. Clearly the Great Pyramid is there mainly because of its size and the labour that must have gone into building it. Large size is indeed something all the Wonders share; none of the Seven Wonders was small, and several of them besides the Great Pyramid – the Temple of Artemis, the Colossus of Rhodes and the Pharos – were among the largest of their kind that have ever been made. But the Temple of Artemis, the Statue of Zeus and the Mausoleum were as famous for their artistic beauty as for their size, while it was the engineering skills that went into the Colossus, the Pharos and the Hanging Gardens that have been most admired.

Why were the Seven Wonders built? The reasons vary. The Hanging Gardens were built for pleasure and the Pharos for a very practical purpose. It is said that the Mausoleum was a queen's memorial to a much loved husband, but it may have been more of a king's memorial to himself. The other four Wonders were built as monuments to religious belief or, as we might say, as great acts of worship or thanksgiving. In the building of all the Wonders there must also have been a feeling of pride and a strong competitive wish to show that the rulers, architects and workmen involved could achieve what others might think impossible.

Sadly, six of the Wonders have gone. The Mausoleum, the Colossus and the Pharos were brought down by earthquakes, and their remains sold or used in other buildings. The Statue of Zeus was destroyed by fire, the Temple of Artemis by human hands on the orders of the Christian Church. The Hanging Gardens disappeared among the ruins of Babylon.

Only the Great Pyramid still stands, in much the same form as it stood 4500 years ago, a truly great Wonder, not only of the Ancient World but of ours too. Just as we marvel at it now, so we can marvel at the others which were great enough to keep it company. Writers who followed Herodotus have described them for us and show us why these were indeed Wonders of the World.

The Great Pyramid at Giza

The only one of the Seven Wonders of the Ancient World that still exists is also the oldest of them all. The Great Pyramid at Giza in Egypt was built some time around 2560 BC; it was already two thousand years old when work began on the next Wonder, the Hanging Gardens of Babylon. The age of the Great Pyramid – more than 4500 years – is so great that it seems almost as if it has been there for ever, and that it will last for ever. In the words of the Arab proverb, 'Man fears Time, but Time fears the Pyramids.'

But age is only one of the reasons why the Great Pyramid is so extraordinary. Another is its size: it is by far the largest of the Seven Wonders and, except for frontier walls such as the Great Wall of China, it is the largest single thing made of stone that has ever been built. Then, too, there is the amazing effort and skill that were needed to cut all that stone and put it together into what is a near-perfect geometrical form, with only simple tools and technology. In fact, if we were asked today for a list of Seven Wonders, ancient or modern, the Great Pyramid would certainly still be on it. But, we may ask, why was such an extraordinary thing ever built? What exactly is it?

The Great Pyramid, like the other larger pyramids in Egypt, is the burial place, or tomb, of one of the country's ancient kings. During the period in Egyptian history known as the Old Kingdom (3100–2180 BC), more than

10

twenty pyramids were built at different places along the River Nile. Three of the larger ones are at Giza, which is now a suburb of Cairo. Like all the other pyramids, they are on the west bank of the Nile, with only the desert and the setting sun beyond. To the ancient Egyptians, the west was the home of the dead. This was where the sun-god Ra, who sailed across the sky in his boat during the day, began his nightly journey down through the Underworld.

For a person's spirit to survive death, the Egyptians believed that the body had to be preserved. This was because the spirit of the dead person left the body at night, but had to return to it in the morning for food and rest. Without these things, the soul would be lost. Members of a family, or their priests, would therefore place food in the tomb of a dead relative, together with furniture and the other necessities of life.

So that the returning spirit would recognize its home, the body had to be kept as life-like as possible, which is why the Egyptians perfected the art of embalming bodies to produce what we now call mummies. We do not know what the ordinary people, who could not afford to pay for embalming, thought would happen to their spirits after their bodies had decayed. Perhaps they simply accepted that, in death as in life, they would not be as lucky as their rulers.

Their king, or pharaoh, was considered to be a god – a son, in fact, of the sun-god Ra – and his body had to be especially well protected after death. We can therefore understand why the pyramid which was his royal tomb was so large: by placing the mummy of the dead pharaoh deep inside such a huge structure, the builders thought that no one would ever be able to disturb it. The shape of the structure was important too: a pyramid represented the rays of the sun as they spread out and touched the earth. The royal tomb was therefore a symbol of the god Ra, the

11

father of the pharaoh. The shape of the tomb may also have represented the way by which the dead pharaoh could join his father. The 'Pyramid Texts', Egypt's earliest religious documents, contain the sentence 'A staircase to heaven is laid for him so that he may climb to heaven thereby.'

Of the three main pyramids at Giza, the largest, the Great Pyramid, was built by Pharaoh Khufu, who is also known as Cheops. It originally rose to a height of 147 metres above the desert sand, but later lost nearly ten

From front to back: the pyramids of Menkaura, Khefren and Khufu.

metres from its pointed top. Not many years later, a second great pyramid appeared beside it, built by Khufu's son Khefren. This pyramid was slightly smaller (144 metres), but Khefren cleverly chose a slightly higher place in the desert for his tomb, so that in fact it looked higher than his father's. (These two pyramids were the tallest buildings in the world for over four thousand years, until the cathedral of the German city of Cologne, which is 157 metres high, was completed in 1880.) The third, and much smaller, pyramid was made for Pharaoh Menkaura. All were probably built within a period of a hundred years.

Near the three pyramids is the famous Sphinx, the strange lion-shaped statue with a human face. It was carved out of natural rock that stands just to the right of the ancient roadway leading to the pyramid of Khefren. It was probably made during this pharaoh's reign and its face may represent that of Khefren himself. Its purpose and meaning are unknown, but even now it seems to lie watchfully guarding the pyramids.

The Great Pyramid was the first of the Giza pyramids to be built, but the sixth in Egypt as a whole. Its builders, who had learnt from the experience and mistakes of the earlier pyramid builders, were extremely exact in their planning and preparation. First, they made the ground level, probably by flooding it and digging it so that the depth of the water was the same everywhere. Then they made the base so that it formed a square with sides almost exactly 229 metres long, with no more than 20 centimetres difference between the longest and shortest sides! Furthermore, the Great Pyramid and its two sister pyramids are placed so that two of their sides face north and south, something that must have been done by observing the stars.

The physical task of building the pyramids has always

The Sphinx and the pyramid of Khefren.

been a subject of great discussion and wonder. They consist
of stone blocks which weigh at least two tonnes each and
often more; and it is estimated that in the Great Pyramid
there are 2.3 million of them. Napoleon Bonaparte, when
resting in the shade of this pyramid after his victory over
the Mamelukes at the Battle of the Pyramids in AD 1798,
calculated that there was enough stone in all three Giza
pyramids to make a wall around the whole of France three
metres high and 30 centimetres thick. (A French
mathematician who was with him is said to have agreed
with his calculation.) How did this huge quantity of stone
get to where it is now?

It was cut out of limestone rock near the River Nile.
Then it was almost certainly floated down the river on
large boats, at the time of the yearly Nile flood, and then
probably along a specially-built canal to a place 600-1000
metres from the building site. From there the blocks were

dragged on wooden rollers along a roadway – of which signs can still be seen – to the pyramid. Then came the task of lifting them into position, higher and higher as the building went on. How this was done is a mystery. Pulleys could not have been used because they had not yet been invented.

It has been suggested that a ramp was built round and round the growing pyramid in a 'square spiral', winding higher and higher as the building rose. But moving the heavy blocks of stone round the corners would have been very awkward, and only one block could have been put into position at a time.

A similar theory suggests that the blocks were moved up a long straight ramp, which was built at right angles to the pyramid. The ramp would have been made higher as the pyramid grew and, so as not to be steep, it would have been gradually lengthened too, until, by the time the builders were working at the top of the pyramid, it stretched far out into the desert.

A rather different idea, put forward by a master builder, is based on the fact that the Giza pyramids rise in a series of one-metre steps, or levels – one metre being the approximate height of each stone block. According to this theory, which the master builder tested, the blocks were raised up the face of the pyramid by means of levers. These would have consisted of wooden poles tipped with metal, which were pushed under one edge of a block while packing material was placed underneath it; the levers would then be used to raise the other side of the block, and so on. In this way, each block would be levered up from one 'step' to the next, until it reached the top level, where it was moved across into its final position. Using this method, several blocks could have been moved up all four faces of the pyramid at the same time.

It is interesting to compare this theory with what the Greek historian Herodotus wrote after he visited Egypt in the fifth centruy BC: 'After laying the stones for the base, they raised the remaining stones to their places by means of machines formed of short wooden planks. The first machine raised them from the ground to the top of the first step. On this there was another machine, which received the stone upon its arrival, and carried it to the second step, from where a third machine advanced it still higher.'

When the 'stepped' pyramid was completed, with the blocks placed so closely and accurately that not even a knife blade could be pushed between them, the builders' task was not over. The angles between the steps were filled in with high-quality white limestone from hills on the eastern side of the River Nile, and this was cut and polished to form a smooth, even slope from top to bottom of the pyramid. The finished result, shining white in the sun, must have looked very different from today's rough, stepped appearance. Some of this special limestone can still be seen near the top of Khefren's pyramid, but it has all gone from the other two, having been taken and used in the building of Cairo. Finally, the pointed top of each pyramid was probably covered in gold, to catch the rays of the sun.

The pyramid shape, with its angle of just under 55 degrees, seems to us so familiar, and perfect, that it is easy to forget that it was not suddenly invented but was the result of a gradual process of trying out different shapes. At least one earlier pyramid, which had more steeply sloping sides, fell down soon after it was built. In another, which is still standing, the slope becomes less steep half-way up, as if the architects suddenly doubted whether the shape they had planned was the right one. It is known as the Bent Pyramid.

A close-up view of the Great Pyramid, showing its stepped appearance.

Herodotus says that it took ten years and 100,000 men to build the Great Pyramid. Diodorus of Sicily, on the other hand, who lived at the time of Julius Caesar, says that it took twenty years and 360,000 men. Whoever is right, it clearly took a great many men a very long time. They probably worked only during the yearly Nile flood, in the summer months from July to October. They would then have been able to move the stone most of the way by boat, and they would also have been free of their work as farmers. Near the bases of the pyramids at Giza one can still see the remains of the 'mini-towns' where the workers lived.

It was often thought that these thousands of workers were used as forced labour, driven by slave-drivers with whips to perform their back-breaking task under a burning sun. The idea was expressed in one or two of the old dramatic Hollywood films about ancient Egypt, but this idea is out of date. It is now thought quite likely that the work on the pyramids was done willingly, out of a sense of religious duty.

It is perhaps difficult nowadays to imagine a society like that of ancient Egypt, where so much time and energy were spent on thinking about and planning for death. What was it like for a young pharaoh and his family to watch work beginning on his own burial place? How did it feel to see that work's slow but sure progress over the years? Was it depressing – or comforting? And was it interesting to take part in discussions with architects on how best to keep one's dead body safe within the pyramid? Trying to answer such questions can only add to the mystery that surrounds the pyramids and their builders.

When Pharaoh Khufu died, his body would have been embalmed, or mummified, and placed in a mummy case. It would then have been brought to the Great Pyramid along the same roadway that had been used for transporting the stone. But the roadway was now given sides and a roof so that priests could bring the body of the god-king privately to the Pyramid Temple which would, by now, have been built at the eastern side of the pyramid. After a special ceremony the body was taken round to the north side where, in all three of the Giza pyramids, there is an entrance into the interior.

In Khefren's pyramid, a passage slopes downwards from this entrance to an underground burial chamber, almost directly beneath the top of the pyramid. The same kind of passage was dug in the Great Pyramid, but the chamber was never finished; instead, a burial chamber was made inside the pyramid about 45 metres above the ground, with

18

a passage sloping up to it. The chamber is large and made of huge blocks of polished granite. In it there was room not only for a stone coffin, or sarcophagus, but for the many articles of furniture that would be needed by the god-king.

After the mummy had been placed in the sarcophagus, and the burial ceremony had been completed, the priests would have left the Great Pyramid by the way they had come. Workmen then closed up the burial chamber by knocking away wooden posts and allowing blocks of granite to fall and slide away from them into the sloping passage. The workmen were able to leave the pyramid by an escape tunnel which runs down into the older underground passage. There was no question of allowing them to share the pyramid with the pharaoh. As they left, they blocked both the tunnel and the passage behind them.

We know, however, that all the labour and care that was taken to preserve and protect for ever the body of the dead pharaoh, son of Ra, was in vain. It seems that, little more than four hundred years after the burial chambers of the Giza pyramids were so carefully closed, robbers succeeded in breaking into them and stealing their contents. These must have included fine objects of gold and ivory, as well as the beautifully-decorated mummy cases. When the British archaeologist Flinders Petrie entered the Great Pyramid in AD 1880, the burial chamber contained no more than the empty sarcophagus. Some people, however, think that this chamber and the empty sarcophagus were cleverly intended to trick any robbers into believing that other robbers had got there before them. According to this theory, Khufu's body and all his rich burial goods may still lie undiscovered somewhere else within the pyramid.

One of the people who is thought to have got there before Petrie was the Caliph Ma'mun, who lived in the ninth century AD. By that time the original entrance to the

19

Great Pyramid had become hidden behind fallen stones, and Ma'mun made another one below it, which is still called Ma'mun's Hole. (It is this entrance which is used by tourists today, although the first one can now be seen.) Some say that Ma'mun found a bird made of gold and a huge precious stone, but it is more likely that he was much too late in his search for treasure and that he found nothing.

The ancient Egyptians went on building pyramids after those at Giza, but none were as large or as well made. Then, during what is called the New Kingdom (1570–1085 BC), pyramid-building stopped. The pharaohs of Egypt – of whom Tutankhamun is the best known – were then buried in tombs made in solid rock in the Valley of the Kings near Thebes (modern Luxor), 500 kilometres south of Giza. It is as if the pharaohs and their advisers at last realized that pyramids, instead of protecting the royal tombs, actually attracted robbers like bees to a hive.

But even in the Valley of the Kings the tombs were not safe, and we know that eventually the priests had to move some royal mummies, under cover of darkness, to even more secret hiding places. Some tombs, however, remained undisturbed until the twentieth century. That of Tutankhamun, who lived around 1350 BC, was not opened until 1925, when the world was able to admire for the first time the beauty and richness which had accompanied the young pharaoh on his last journey.

Even at the Great Pyramid something remained undiscovered until as late as 1954. In that year a young Egyptian archaeologist, Kamul al-Mallakh, found, in a large hole close to the south side of the pyramid and beneath large blocks of limestone, a wooden boat 40 metres long. It is made of 1274 separate pieces fitted together without the use of a single metal nail, and is complete with a cabin and oars. This, then, is what King Khufu's people made for him so that he could travel with his father, the sun-god Ra, across the heavens. The 'sun boat' now lies in a museum built especially for it near the Great Pyramid.

As for Khufu himself, although we may never know what became of his body, his name will be remembered as long as the Great Pyramid still stands – a monument both to him and to the achievements of which human beings are capable.

Dates

BC

3100–2180	Period of the Old Kingdom in ancient Egypt.
2670	First pyramid begun near Memphis: 70 metres high.
2550–2520	Reign of King Khufu; building of the Great Pyramid.
2150–2050	Giza pyramids robbed.
1570–1085	New Kingdom; kings buried at Thebes (Luxor).
450	Herodotus visits Egypt.

AD

850	Caliph Ma'mun enters the Great Pyramid.
1798	Napoleon at the Pyramids.
1880	Flinders Petrie enters the Great Pyramid.
1954	King Khufu's boat found by Kamal al-Mallakh.

Measurements

Age of Great Pyramid:	about 4550 years
Original height:	146.6 metres
Length of side at base:	229 metres
Angle of slope:	54.5 degrees
Estimated number of stone blocks:	2,300,000
Weight of each block:	2 tonnes minimum

The Hanging Gardens of Babylon

The remains of the city of Babylon are now in Iraq, about 150 kilometres south of present-day Baghdad. The city was at one time the splendid capital of an empire. Its position on both banks of the River Euphrates, which has a fertile flood plain, made it rich in agricultural produce. This was traded with foreign nations for precious metals and stones, and for ivory, silk and wood. The Babylonian empire was at its greatest in about 600 BC, when it stretched from the coast of the Mediterranean in the west to the border of Persia in the east; and from the River Tigris in the north to the Arabian desert in the south.

We know a good deal about this empire and its well-developed civilization and culture. This is because the Babylonian language, Akkadian, was written as well as spoken. Its writing system, known as cuneiform, was made up of triangle-like marks cut in pieces of clay or stone, many of which have been found. After much hard work by scholars in the nineteenth century, Akkadian can now be understood and translated. The result is that, as well as examples of Babylonian literature, we have written evidence of what went on in everyday society.

There are, for example, records of government and business activities, from which we know that the Babylonians invented a system of weights and measures which was later used by the Greeks and Romans. We know, too, of the

Babylonians' deep interest in astronomy and astrology. These subjects were closely connected with their religion, which was of great importance to them. Each city had its own chief god or goddess who was worshipped at his or her special temple. The god of the city of Babylon was Bel, or Marduk, who was the king of the gods, the Babylonian equivalent of the Greek god Zeus.

More than once in the history of Babylon, Bel's statue made of gold was stolen from his temple in time of war, and the Babylonians had to fight to recover it. The Greek historian Herodotus visited Babylon around 450 BC and writes that he saw this statue together with its golden throne and a table of gold beside it. He was, he says, told that 22 tonnes of gold were used to make them.

Babylon's most famous king was Nebuchadnezzar II, who ruled from 605 to 562 BC. His father Nabopolassar had, with the help of the kingdom of Media to his north, finally freed Babylon from the power of the Assyrians and had destroyed Nineveh, their capital city on the River Tigris. Nebuchadnezzar went on to replace the Assyrian empire with his own. In 586 BC he destroyed Jerusalem and removed its Jewish inhabitants to Babylon as slaves. When he was not fighting, Nebuchadnezzar spent his energy on rebuilding his capital so that it became, in the opinion of Herodotus, the finest city in the world.

As in ancient Egypt, the chief building material in Babylon was mud bricks. Like the River Nile, the Euphrates overflowed its banks each spring; bricks were then easily made by shaping the mud and leaving it to dry in the hot sun. Using millions of these bricks, the royal architects added to the city walls already begun by Nebuchadnezzar's father and built magnificent gates, palaces and temples.

The walls, which completely enclosed the city, are said to have been 23 metres high and nearly ten metres thick, so that there was room on the top for two four-horse chariots side by side. In fact, the city walls became so famous that at one time they were included, as well as the Hanging Gardens, in the list of the Seven Wonders. They had eight gates, the most famous of which was the Ishtar Gate on the north side of the city, near the eastern bank of the river. The gates, like many of the buildings, were beautifully decorated with carvings of lions, bulls and other animals on a background of blue bricks.

Within the walls, wide straight streets were laid out parallel with the Euphrates flowing through the middle of the city; others crossed them at right angles. The finest street was the Processional Way, which ran straight across the city from the Ishtar Gate. Just inside this gate, and between the Processional Way and the river, Nebuchadnezzar built the largest palace that had ever been seen in that part of the world; it was larger than the Assyrian palace at Nineveh, and even larger than the palace which the Persian King Xerxes built at Persepolis in the following century. It covered an area of five hectares and was built around five large courtyards.

It was here, near the palace and next to the river, that the famous Hanging Gardens of Babylon probably stood. They did not 'hang' in the proper sense of the word: they 'hung' only in the sense that they appeared well above the heads of people looking at them from ground level or from the river. This was because the Gardens were planted on terraces which rose one behind the other, so that the highest was level with the top of the city wall that ran along the river's eastern bank. The story – which may or may not be true – is that Nebuchadnezzar made them to please his young wife, a princess called Amytis from the mountainous kingdom of Media, to the north of Babylonia. On the dull, flat plain of the Euphrates she felt homesick for the trees and mountains of her homeland.

The change from dry brick courtyards and walls to a green mountainside with trees and flowers, with cool green shade and perhaps the sound of running water, must have seemed like a miracle. But beautiful gardens in the middle of

An artist's impression of the Hanging Gardens.

that desert region were certainly not unknown. The kings of the fallen empire of Assyria had been very proud of theirs, and took a great deal of trouble to water them. They left descriptions of them cut in stone, including lists of plants, and Assurbanipal (668–627 BC), the last great Assyrian king, had a picture carved of his garden at Nineveh which is now in the British Museum.

The terraces of the Hanging Gardens of Babylon were supported by stone columns resting on walls six metres thick with three metres between them. On top of the columns there lay stone beams, five metres long and three metres wide. Above these was a waterproof layer of reeds mixed with bitumen, then a layer of brick, and finally one of lead. Last of all came earth, with was deep enough 'for the roots of trees ... of every kind that, by their great size or any other charm, could give pleasure to whoever looks on them.' There were 'machines for supplying the Gardens with water ... although no one outside could see it being done.'

We owe this description to Diodorus of Sicily, who lived in the first century BC. Fairly full descriptions like this one have come down to us from three other ancient writers, including the Greek writer Strabo, who lived from 64 BC to AD 24. They are all in general agreement about what they describe, and were all clearly full of wonder at what they had heard about the Gardens; for it is doubtful whether any of these writers actually saw them. (Three of them lived at a time when Babylon was already falling into ruins.) The only writer who would have seen them if they were there was Herodotus. But he does not mention them.

It is possible that when Herodotus was in Babylon, so carefully describing what he saw, the Gardens built by Nebuchadnezzar no longer existed. The trees and plants may have been destroyed or left to die when the city became part of the Persian empire in 539 BC. The Gardens may have been replanted by the time Alexander the Great entered the city as conqueror of the Persians in 331 BC; or when he later decided to make Babylon the magnificent capital of his huge empire. However, when Alexander died in 323 BC – in the very palace that Nebuchadnezzar had built – his empire broke up, and the city that was to have been his capital was quite soon left empty and forgotten.

Like the sites of some of the other Seven Wonders, Babylon remained undisturbed in the dust of time until archaeologists began digging in its ruins at the end of the last century. So far they have discovered no clear proof of the existence of the Hanging Gardens. In fact, what has been dug up has only added to the mystery left by Herodotus. Cuneiform texts have been found which are a careful record of the building work done in Babylon during the reign of Nebuchadnezzar. They list the streets that were laid out, and the gates, temples, palaces and other buildings that were put up or repaired. Clearly the king wished to make known what had been done in his name. But nowhere are the Hanging Gardens mentioned.

Who, then, told us that the Gardens were made by Nebuchadnezzar? It was a Babylonian called Berossus, who lived in the time of Alexander the Great. He also tells us that they had been built for the Princess Amytis. The idea that this powerful king made them to please his young queen struck a romantic note which has sounded through the centuries. It originated in the book which Berossus wrote in Greek about Babylonian culture and civilization and which, although now lost, has been quoted by other writers.

So, like the Gardens, we are left 'hanging' in some doubt as to whether they were built by Nebuchadnezzar, and perhaps even whether they existed at all. Neither of the sources we would most expect to mention them – the royal records in cuneiform and the writings of Herodotus – does so.

27

And so far nothing has been found in the ruins of Babylon which can definitely be said to be their remains.

Nevertheless, two thoughts may persuade us that the Hanging Gardens of Babylon did indeed exist: first, that four well-known ancient writers have left us fairly full descriptions of them, which, in general, agree with each other; and, secondly, that the rulers of Babylon would surely have wished to equal other cities such as Nineveh in possessing splendid gardens. When the Hanging Gardens existed, and for how long, would then be the remaining question.

In 1980 the Department of Antiquities in Iraq began to recreate Babylon in order to give back to the city some of the glory it had in the time of Nebuchadnezzar II. Streets are being laid out and walls, temples and palaces are being rebuilt. Over sixty million mud bricks have so far been used, some of them bearing the name of the Iraqi leader Saddam Hussein. (These will no doubt be discovered with great interest by archaeologists in centuries to come.) On rising ground within the city, trees will be planted. If Babylon did not, after all, have its Hanging Gardens in the past, it seems that it will have them in the future.

Dates

BC

625–605	Reign of King Nabopolassar of Babylon.
606	Fall of the Assyrian empire; Nineveh destroyed.
605–562	Reign of Nabopolassar's son, Nebuchadnezzar II.
	Probable construction of the Hanging Gardens.
539	Babylon becomes part of the Persian empire.
450?	Greek historian Herodotus visits Babylon.
331	Alexander the Great enters Babylon as conqueror.

AD

1899	Archaeologists begin to excavate Babylon.
1980	Iraqi government begins to rebuild Babylon.

The Statue of Zeus at Olympia

For most people a visit to ancient Olympia in southern Greece is an unforgettable experience. Olympia was the home of the Greek Olympic Games, and visitors today find that it has a special magic. If you stand in this green and peaceful place, surrounded by wooded hills and the smell of pine trees, your imagination can take you back more than two thousand years. You can almost hear the shouts of the crowds as a winning runner crosses the finishing line. You can imagine the excitement as athletes and their trainers, from all over the ancient Greek world, prepare to take part in the running races and other contests such as wrestling, boxing, horseback and chariot racing, and the pentathlon.

The Olympic Games were so important to the Greeks that they took the date of one of the early ones (776 BC) as the beginning of their calendar. The Games took place every four years until AD 394, that is, for more than a thousand years. It is important to realize that, unlike our modern Olympic Games, those in ancient Greece were religious events, and formed part of a three-month-long festival in honour of Zeus, the principal god of the ancient Greeks, the father and ruler of mankind.

People came from every part of the Greek world, which included cities in Spain, Italy and Africa. They came to worship and to offer gifts to Zeus, and to watch or take part in the Games, which took place during the last five days of the festival, at the time of the August full moon. It may surprise us that the Games were held at the hottest time of the year, but by the month of August most farming work was over and people had more free time. Those who took part in the Games had to be of Greek birth; they prayed to Zeus and other gods to help them to win and, if they won, gave gifts to the god who had helped them. This was often a bronze or marble statue of the athlete himself.

The ruins of the Gymnasium at Olympia.

During the festival, a truce was declared throughout Greece so that people could travel to Olympia in safety. The various Greek city states were often at war, but while the Sacred Truce lasted, all fighting between the states ceased. Anyone who broke the truce had to pay a fine. Once Alexander the Great himself had to pay a fine because some of his soldiers had robbed an Athenian who was travelling to the Games. At first the truce lasted for one month, but later it was extended so that people could come to the Games from further away.

There were three other major athletic festivals in Greece, but the Olympic Games were the oldest and the most important. The Games in the valley of Nemea south of Corinth were also in honour of Zeus; those at Corinth itself were for the god Poseidon; and those at Delphi were for Apollo. Women were not allowed to take part in any of these Games, or even to watch them; if they were found there, the punishment was death. But they had their own Games, also held every four years, in honour of the goddess Hera. The only woman allowed to be present at the Olympic festival was Hera's priestess.

Olympia takes its name from Mount Olympus, about 300 kilometres away in northern Greece. The Greeks believed that the mountain was the home of Zeus and the other gods. So why did Olympia, which is in the southern part of Greece now called the Peloponnese, become his most sacred shrine? The reason was that, according to legend, Zeus chose it himself by using his main weapon, lightning. He threw a thunderbolt from his throne on Mount Olympus and a Great Altar to him was built on the exact spot where it landed, on the banks of the River Alphaeus.

Even before the Great Altar at Olympia was built, people worshipped Zeus on the fertile plain there, between the River Alphaeus and the hill of Cronus, named after Zeus's father. In an opening among the trees people had first worshipped the Earth goddess Gaea, the grandmother of Zeus. Later they worshipped Hera, who was his wife, and Zeus himself. They built altars to these and other gods and called the place the Altis. In about 600 BC a large temple was built there to Hera, and in it were placed statues of both her and Zeus.

The Great Altar to Zeus became the most important of the altars in the Altis. It consisted of a simple stone platform with steps leading up to it. On top was a huge pile, several metres high, of the ashes of animals which had been sacrificed and burnt. The ashes were mixed with water from the river and then added to the pile. The most important day of the Olympic Games was the third day of the five, immediately after the full moon, when one hundred oxen were sacrificed at this altar. The animals were taken there in a splendid procession of athletes, Olympic judges, and important visitors.

Today there is a small town called Olympia near the site of the ancient Games. But in ancient times the only people who lived there were the priests who looked after the altars and temple and the religious part of the festival. The Games themselves were under the control of the people of Elis, the region in which Olympia was situated. The city of Elis was about 50 kilometres away, and it was there that the athletes had to stay for a month's training before the Games began. Then, just two days before, they set out with their trainers and the judges to Olympia. At the same time, all sorts of other people were travelling to Olympia, including representatives of the Greek city states, and craftsmen and merchants. Some came on foot, others by horse or chariot, and some came by boat the fifteen kilometres up the River Alphaeus from the coast.

In the fifth century BC, when the Games were becoming more and more important, the people of Elis decided to build a new temple for Zeus alone. Until then, as we have seen, the statue of Zeus shared a temple with that of Hera, his wife. It was Hera, rather than Zeus, who was worshipped by the people of the regions near Elis, and the Eleans (the citizens of Elis) probably wished to show that Zeus was the greatest god. The best way to do this was to build a temple so large and magnificent that the god's power would be clear to anyone who saw it.

It took the Eleans about ten years to complete the new

temple, which was designed by Libon, one of their own architects. A building of this size and magnificence was clearly very expensive, but they managed to pay for it with riches they had won in war. The temple was built of huge stone blocks, with a roof supported by 34 great columns in the simple Doric style. The triangular ends of the roof were decorated with splendid sculptures of mythological scenes, and the roof tiles were of a special kind of marble brought from near Athens. The finished temple was the largest in the Peloponnese and, because it received so many visitors during the Olympic festival, its fame soon grew.

The main purpose of a Greek temple was to provide a home for a statue of the god in whose honour the temple was built. But for twenty years the magnificent new temple built for Zeus at Olympia was without a suitable statue. Finally the Eleans decided to have one made which would be as magnificent as the temple itself. To do this, they chose Phidias of Athens. Born around 490 BC, he had become the most famous Greek sculptor of his time and he is now considered to have been the greatest sculptor of ancient Greece.

Phidias had recently been in charge of the building of the Parthenon, the temple of the goddess Athena on the hill called the Acropolis in Athens. Besides sculptures on the temple itself, he had made two very large statues of Athena. One, made of bronze and almost ten metres high, could be seen far out to sea by sailors leaving or returning home; the other, made of gold and ivory, stood inside the Parthenon. In 438 BC Phidias left Athens for Olympia, over 200 kilometres away, to begin work on his next great statue. It, too, was to be of gold and ivory. And it was to become one of the Seven Wonders of the World.

Pausanias, the Greek writer of a travellers' guide to Greece, visited Olympia in AD 174, and it is to him that we owe a full description of the finished statue. The enormous

33

figure of Zeus sat on a magnificent throne made of black ebony wood. The statue was thirteen metres tall – seven times as tall as a man – so tall, in fact, that the god's head was only a metre away from the ceiling of the temple. Ivory was used for the god's flesh, and gold for his robe, which was

An artist's impression of the statue of Zeus.

An eighteenth-century artist's impression of the statue and part of the temple.

decorated with animals and flowers. In his right hand he held a small statue of the winged goddess Victory; in his left he held the symbol of his kingship, a royal sceptre, with an eagle on top. Both the statue and the sceptre were made of ivory, gold and other metals. The god's feet, in gold sandals, rested on a footstool guarded by gold lions; his head was crowned with olive branches.

The throne, in the opinion of Pausanias, was just as wonderful as the statue of Zeus itself. It was so beautifully decorated and carved with scenes from Greek mythology that Pausanias was in no doubt that it, too, was the work of Phidias. The base of blue-black marble on which the throne stood was nearly seven metres wide and over a metre high, and was decorated in gold with more scenes from mythology. In front of the base, where the floor was of the same blue-black marble, there was a shallow basin with a white marble edge. This was filled with olive oil which from time to time was poured over the statue, probably to keep the parts made of ivory in good condition.

The pool of olive oil must also have served as a mirror which reflected light from the doorway of the temple onto the statue. There were no windows, and the statue stood at the back of the building. There was a raised gallery running round the inside of the temple, which visitors could use to obtain a better view of the upper part of the statue. But whether they saw this amazing piece of sculpture from above or below, its size and magnificence must have had a great effect on them, especially in the shadowy light of the temple; and some must have felt that they were in the presence of the great god Zeus himself.

For the ancient Greeks, Zeus was a god with more than one side to his character. He was not only the all-powerful king and ruler of gods and men, the maker of thunder and lightning who could produce storms with one shake of his sceptre. He was also the protector of cities, the god of friendship and hospitality, and a loving father who looked after his worshippers and gave them riches. In a speech made at the Olympic Games of AD 97, Phidias was praised for having shown all these different qualities together in the one statue.

But how was it actually made? The statue of Athena in the Parthenon had been made by laying gold and ivory on top of a wooden frame made in the shape of the goddess. Phidias used the same method at Olympia: thin sheets of ivory for the god's skin and hammered gold for his clothing were shaped and fixed to the massive wooden frame that had been made in the form of the seated god; and this was done so carefully that no joins could be seen. But, whereas in Athens Phidias had worked in the temple of the Parthenon itself, at Olympia he built a large workshop about a hundred metres from the temple and made the statue there.

Pausanias saw this workshop on his visit in AD 174. Later a Christian church, which still exists, was built on top of the workshop floor. Archaeologists now think that this floor would not have been strong enough to support the huge weight of the statue and the throne, and so it is believed that the work was carried out in stages, and that the separate pieces were put together in the temple. Fortunately for us, Phidias and his workmen left a large amount of rubbish near the workshop, and this was found by German archaeologists in the 1950s. It included pieces of ivory as well as tools of bronze and bone. The most exciting discovery, though, was a piece of broken jug marked with the words 'I belong to Phidias'.

The sculptor spent five or six years working on his statue. A story tells how, after finishing it, he prayed to Zeus to ask whether the statue pleased him and was answered with a flash of lightning, which he understood to mean 'Yes'. But Phidias was not so well received in Athens when he returned there in 432 BC. He was accused of having made one of the sculptures in the Parthenon look like himself, and of stealing some of the gold provided for the statue of Athena. Some say that he was made to leave the city, others that he was imprisoned, or even executed – a tragic end for such a great artist.

His statue, however, remained within its temple at Olympia for more than eight hundred years. In the first century AD, when Greece had become part of the Roman empire, the emperor Caligula wanted to have the statue taken to Rome and to replace its head with a copy of his own; but it is said that, when workmen were getting ready to move it out of the temple, the statue gave such a loud laugh that the huge framework they had built for its transportation broke, causing them to run away in terror. The reign of the evil Caligula was short (AD 37–41), and the statue was soon safe again.

In AD 391, however, Theodosius I made Christianity the official religion of the Roman empire and forbade the worship of all pagan gods. The Olympic Games were stopped, and the temple of Zeus at Olympia was closed. In AD 426 the emperor Theodosius II had the statue of Zeus transported to his palace in Constantinople (now Istanbul), where it might have remained to this day. But less than fifty years later a fire destroyed the royal palace, together with what had already been called one of the Seven Wonders of the Ancient World.

Olympia, meanwhile, was becoming deserted. In the sixth century the River Alphaeus changed its course and the temple of Zeus was destroyed by earthquakes and floods. The whole area became covered in sand and mud and remained so until 1829, when archaeologists began to uncover the remains of the great temple. These remains can now be seen, either at the site itself or in a local museum, together with the finds from Phidias' workshop.

Dates

BC

776	First recorded Olympic Games.
456–446	Temple of Zeus built at Olympia.
438–432	Phidias makes the statue of Zeus.

AD

391	Theodosius I closes the temple and stops the Games.
426	Theodosius II takes the statue to Constantinople.
475	Statue of Zeus destroyed by fire.
1829	First archaeological excavations at Olympia.
1896	First modern Olympic Games, in Athens.

Measurements

Height of statue of Zeus:	13 metres
Height of temple ceiling:	14 metres
Size of base of statue:	10 metres by 6.5 metres by 1 metre
Area of base of temple:	64 metres by 27 metres

The Temple of Artemis at Ephesus

Every year thousands of tourists visit the ruined city of
Ephesus on the west coast of Turkey near the modern town
of Selçuk. Few of them, however, have the time or energy
to make their way in the summer heat to the site of the
ancient temple of Artemis, some way from the main ruins.

The ruins of the temple, with the Byzantine Basilica of St John.

If they do, there is sadly very little to see: one lonely column reaching to the sky and a few broken pieces of stone are all that remain of what was judged to be the most magnificent Greek temple in the world.

Ephesus was the most important of the twelve settlements made by ancient Greeks on the coast of Anatolia and its offshore islands. By the second century AD the city had a population of 300,000, and was the capital of the Roman province of Asia and a busy seaport. It was also the centre of the worship of the goddess Artemis, and the thousands of worshippers who went there brought great wealth to the city. But who was Artemis, and why did the people of Ephesus build such a large and beautiful temple in her honour?

It is important to remember that, although ancient Ephesus was a Greek city, its people were also affected by the customs and religions of their Anatolian neighbours. In Greek mythology, Artemis was the goddess of youth and was usually shown as a huntress, often with her dogs. She was the daughter of Zeus and twin sister of Apollo, and became known to the Romans as Diana. But the Artemis whom people worshipped at Ephesus was more like the Anatolian goddess of fertility called the Great Mother, or Cybele.

Roman copies of statues of the Artemis of Ephesus, together with her image on coins, show us what she looked like. The lower part of her body was straight like a pillar, tightly clothed in a long skirt covered with animals and bees. (The bee was the symbol of Ephesus.) Above her waist hung more than a dozen egg-like shapes – scholars disagree about whether they represent eggs, female breasts, grapes or some other fruit. Whatever they are, the idea of fertility which they express, with the bees and animals, is very clear.

40

A Roman statue of Artemis of Ephesus (1st century AD).

Fertility in agriculture was even more important in the ancient world, when transport was difficult, than it is now; the life of a community depended on it. This eastern Artemis was the giver of fertility, the mother and ruler of nature. On her head she wore a tall crown, and her arms were stretched out like those of a woman towards her child. So the Ephesians – and, as time went on, more and

41

more visitors – worshipped her and prayed to her to protect their animals and crops.

It is impossible to say when the worship of the Ephesian Artemis began, but the first known altar or shrine was built about 700 BC. The very first object of worship was not a statue but a large stone – perhaps a meteorite – which people said had fallen from the sky six hundred years earlier. By the sixth century BC the worship of Artemis had become so important to the Ephesians that they decided to build a great temple in her honour. The architects they chose came from the island of Crete and had just completed a magnificent new temple to the goddess Hera on the island of Samos. The one they built at Ephesus was begun in 564 BC.

The site was on soft ground near the mouth of the River Cayster, but the architects were experienced in building in such places. To make the foundations of the temple firm, they filled the wetter places on the one-hectare site with alternate layers of charcoal and sheepskins – an unusual technique but apparently very successful. The design of the temple itself was ambitious. In fact we are told that the piece of stone to go over the doorway was so enormous that the chief architect, Chersiphon, had no idea how to lift it, and thought of killing himself in despair. Fortunately, the story says, Artemis herself came to help, and the stone was somehow or other lifted into place.

In 560 BC, while the temple was still being built, the city of Ephesus was attacked by King Croesus, the ruler of the neighbouring province of Lydia. In desperation, the Ephesians joined their city to the temple by a rope, hoping that this would persuade the goddess to defend them. But she failed to do so, and the Lydians entered the city as conquerors. However, Artemis had not really abandoned the Ephesians. To their surprise, King Croesus, who was an admirer of Greek culture and a worshipper of the goddess, gave them money towards the new temple and a gift of gold statues of bulls to place inside. The grateful citizens had his name carved on the temple columns so that his generosity would be remembered for as long as the temple stood.

Unfortunately it lasted less than two hundred years. In 356 BC a man called Herostratus set fire to it and it burned to the ground. (It seems that part of the temple was made of wood.) The reason Herostratus gave for this terrible deed was that he wanted everlasting fame, which he achieved in a strange kind of way: afterwards the Ephesians punished with death anyone who said his name, which came to mean 'wicked'. They were horrified at the loss of their temple. Apart from the terrible insult to their goddess, they must also have worried about the effect on trade, since so much of their wealth came from the visitors who worshipped Artemis.

The thing the citizens clearly had to do was to replace the temple as soon as possible, and this they set about doing. But it took them about fifty years. In 334 BC, twenty-two years after the fire, Alexander the Great visited the city and saw the new temple being built. He knew that the name of King Croesus had been on the columns of the earlier building, and wanted to be given the same honour. He offered to pay the whole cost of the new building if his own name was put on it. But the Ephesians politely refused, saying that it was not right that one god should make gifts to another.

Did they perhaps really believe that Alexander – who had, after all, just won his first brilliant victory against the powerful Persians – was in fact a god? Perhaps they did, because it was said later that the reason Artemis had not been able to save her first great temple from destruction was that Alexander was born on the very same night that it was burnt down; she was therefore away in Macedonia seeing that all went well at his birth. (Being the goddess of fertility meant that she was also the goddess of childbirth.)

The new temple, when finished, was a magnificent building of shining white marble which the Roman writer

An artist's impression of the later Temple of Artemis.

Pliny the Elder has described for us. It was on a high marble base 131 metres long and 78 metres wide. Thirteen steps led up to it on all four sides. Rising from the base in two rows, one behind the other, was a forest of 127 beautiful columns in the Ionic style. These were 19 metres high and 36 of them were decorated with brightly painted carvings.

The fame of the new temple grew, and it was soon recognized as the finest Greek temple in the world. It was also one of the largest, being nearly twice the size of the Parthenon in Athens. The roof was so wide that a space had to be left in the middle to reduce the weight on the supporting columns. Inside the temple there was a special room where the statue of Artemis was kept. Alexander was so impressed by the work of the architect, Deinocrates, that he later asked him to design Alexandria, his new city in Egypt.

As the temple grew in importance, the number of priests, priestesses and guards increased until there were several hundred of them. Twenty of these priests formed a special group called 'acrobats' who did complicated dances during the religious ceremonies. Since the temple was so well guarded – and because few people would have dared to rob it anyway – it was also used as a kind of bank for money. The chief priest, who was in charge of the many gifts made to the temple, had the power to make loans to people in return.

High up over the main entrance to the temple, in the triangular end to the roof, were three windows, a large one in the middle and two smaller ones on either side. Such windows were unusual in Greek temples, but more common in Anatolian ones. On certain occasions, the statue of Artemis would appear at the central window to be shown to her faithful worshippers standing in the great courtyard below, while the priests sacrificed animals to her at the open-air altar. Afterwards, pieces of the sacrificial meat were sold and eaten, hot from the altar fire. At other times the temple courtyard became a busy market-place, where people bought and sold goods, including, among other things, small silver and gold copies of the statue and the temple.

Once a year, on her birthday, the statue of Artemis was taken out of the temple and carried in a great procession to the amphitheatre, to be present at special games held in her honour. The event was celebrated with music and dancing, and with the sacrifice of animals. One writer in the first century AD has left us a description of this festival, in which he says that the smoke from the sacrifices was so thick that he could not see the sun.

Both the earlier and the new temple were well known for their law of asylum, which meant that anyone, even a criminal, whose life was in danger could go there to seek the protection of the chief priest. It was said that among the first seekers of asylum were some of the warlike women living near the Black Sea, called Amazons. Whether there really were such people or not, they were important in Greek mythology, and battles between Greeks and Amazons were often shown in sculpture. In the fifth century BC a competition was held called the Amazon Statue Competition: the most famous sculptors of the time were invited to create a bronze statue of an Amazon to decorate the first temple of Artemis.

One of the sculptors who entered the competition was Phidias, who later made the famous statue of Zeus at Olympia. But, perhaps surprisingly, he was not the winner. The sculptors themselves were asked to judge the competition, and they each chose their own statue as the best, and a statue by a sculptor called Polycleitus as second best. So Polycleitus won. His statue and three others, including the one by Phidias, were placed near or above the entrance to the temple. Unfortunately, none of these statues have survived, but there are many Roman copies of them in museums.

As time went on, various people, some famous, sought asylum at the temple of Artemis. When the Persian King Xerxes was finally defeated in his war with the Greeks in 479 BC, he sent his children there, fearing for their safety. A tragic event occurred in 41 BC concerning Arsinoe, the younger sister of the famous Queen Cleopatra of Egypt. Ephesus was by then within the Roman empire, and Arsinoe's life was in danger from Mark Antony, Cleopatra's Roman lover, who feared that Arsinoe would take the throne of Egypt from her elder sister. She fled for safety to the temple, but Mark Antony forced the chief priest to bring her out. He then had her murdered to make sure that power in Egypt remained with Cleopatra and himself.

It is strange that Mark Antony broke the law of asylum in this way because he himself had doubled the size of the sacred area around the temple of Artemis to include part of the city. Enlarging the area of asylum was something that new rulers often did. Alexander the Great had done this when he freed Ephesus from the Persians, and Mark Antony no doubt wished to show that he could do even better. The Ephesians, however, soon began to dislike the law of asylum because it encouraged criminals to come to Ephesus. In AD 22 they asked the Roman emperor Tiberius to change the law, but he refused.

In AD 52 the Christian teacher Saint Paul arrived in Ephesus from Corinth. He continued to teach at Ephesus for three winters, speaking against the worship of Artemis, saying that 'gods made with human hands are not gods at all'. A silversmith named Demetrius became worried that, if Christianity grew, the craftsmen like himself who made model statues and temples would lose the trade that depended upon the ancient religion. He stirred up the people, who gathered in a great crowd in the amphitheatre, seizing two of Paul's travelling companions and shouting, 'Great is Artemis of the Ephesians!' An official of the city succeeded in calming them, however, and soon afterwards Paul left the region.

Although their old religion was now being threatened by a new one, the Ephesians continued to worship at the temple of Artemis at least until the end of the fourth century AD. In AD 263 the temple was badly damaged by Goths invading Anatolia from the north. But the determined Ephesians repaired it. Finally, however, in AD 391 the Christian emperor Theodosius I ordered it, and all other pagan temples within the Roman empire, to be closed, and ten years later, John Chrysostom, the Archbishop of Constantinople, had it destroyed.

In the sixth century some of the temple stones were used in the building of a large Christian church nearby; and some of the sculptures were taken to Constantinople (now Istanbul) by Emperor Justinian, to decorate the Byzantine church of Hagia Sofia. The rest of the temple sank deeper and deeper beneath the mud which was brought down by the River Cayster and which slowly filled the port of Ephesus. The city itself fell into ruins. By the time the remains of the temple were discovered by a British archaeologist in the 1860s, they were over four metres below ground.

It is said, however, that in spite of what happened to their temple, the people of Ephesus continued for many centuries to worship their beloved goddess in the form of simple stones recovered from the sacred site, just as they had first worshipped her when she fell from the sky.

Dates

BC

700 ?	First known altar to Artemis.
564	Building of the first great temple begins.
356	Herostratus burns down the temple.
334	Alexander the Great sees the new temple being built.

AD

52	Saint Paul at Ephesus.
263	Temple partly destroyed by Goths.
391	Theodosius I orders all pagan temples to be closed.
401	John Chrysostom orders the destruction of the temple.
1863	Excavations begin on the site of the temple.

Measurements

Length of temple:	131 metres
Width of temple:	78.5 metres
Number of columns:	127
Height of columns:	19 metres

The Mausoleum at Halicarnassus

Very few speakers of English realize that the word *mausoleum*, meaning a large, splendid tomb, comes from the name of a real person – King Mausolus, ruler of Caria. When he died in 353 BC, the tomb he was buried in was called the Mausoleum. It was the finest building in his capital city of Halicarnassus, which is now Bodrum, a busy town on the coast of south-western Turkey. A visitor today who wished to see the tomb would be disappointed, for very little of it remains. The magnificent monument in stone to King Mausolus has gone; but the word *mausoleum* has kept his name alive.

Halicarnassus was founded by Greeks in the eleventh century BC. The site was a good place to choose for a coastal town: there were surrounding hills to give shelter, a perfect natural harbour, and good agricultural land nearby. It soon became the chief town of the region of Caria. However, Halicarnassus did not remain independent for long. In the seventh century BC it fell to the kings of Lydia. Then, when King Croesus of Lydia was defeated by the Persians in 546 BC, Caria with the city of Halicarnassus became part of the huge Persian empire. From then on, the rulers of Caria were governors, or satraps, for the Persians.

In the year 377 BC Mausolus became governor of Caria. Although he was not an independent ruler, Caria was a long way from the centres of Persian government in Susa or

Babylon and, as long as there was peace in the region, the Persians were happy to leave Mausolus alone. So he was free to rule more or less as he wished and, since he had the necessary wealth, he was able to do much to satisfy his desire for power and fame. As we shall see, Mausolus was a man who did things on a grand scale.

First of all he decided to move his capital from Mylasa, where his father had ruled, to Halicarnassus, about 40 kilometres away. He then set about rebuilding it to make it the kind of capital city he wanted. He deepened and improved the harbour to make room for his fleet of one hundred warships. He had fine new streets and squares planned and laid out in the Greek style. He built a massive fortified palace, of brick covered with marble, in a safe position on one side of the harbour, where a castle now stands. And around his splendid new capital he built a wall over five kilometres long with watchtowers. The city was now protected on all sides.

What was still missing was people, for although the city was now much larger in area, the population had not grown with it. To solve this problem, Mausolus simply forced thousands of his people to move to Halicarnassus from other parts of Caria, and in this way made its population five times larger. Halicarnassus was now a fine city, suitable for a king. Mausolus had thought about entertainment too, and had built a Greek-style theatre on a hillside overlooking the harbour. He had not forgotten the gods either, and had built a temple.

It is interesting that he chose to dedicate this temple to Ares, the Greek god of war. In Greek mythology, Ares sometimes helped the enemies of his own people. Mausolus may have had this in mind when he dedicated the temple because, as a governor for the Persians, he was guarding the western frontier of their empire against the Greeks, his main enemy. And yet he and his citizens greatly admired, and copied, Greek culture.

As Halicarnassus became established as the capital, and taxes poured in from all over Caria, Mausolus and his wife Artemisia were able to spend their wealth on making the city even more beautiful. They employed the best architects and craftsmen, and more temples, statues, and other fine buildings were added. But the most impressive of them all had not yet appeared – the king's own tomb, a monument to his glory. The royal couple chose the best site in the centre of the city for what was to become the most splendid tomb of its kind that has ever been built. When the Roman writer Pliny the Elder described the Mausoleum in AD 75, it was already regarded as one of the Seven Wonders of the World.

According to Pliny, the whole tomb was 43 metres high and divided into three sections. The base was roughly square, with sides about 33 metres long. He does not give the height of this bottom section, but it was probably about 20 metres. On top of this was what looked like a Greek temple, with nine to eleven columns on each of the four sides. The roof, or third section, did not look Greek at all: it was a pyramid rising in 24 steps to a flat top on which stood a chariot pulled by four horses. We know from the remains that most of the tomb was solid, with green volcanic stone inside and white marble outside.

The most beautiful feature of the Mausoleum was the many wonderful sculptures which decorated it, and it was almost certainly these, and not just the monument's size, which led people to call it one of the Seven Wonders. The statues and carvings were the work of five different Greek sculptors, of whom the most famous was Scopas from the island of Paros. The fact that Mausolus saw the Greeks as his political enemies did not, as we have already noted, stop him admiring the work of their craftsmen. Nor did it prevent him employing them if they were the best.

Four of these sculptors each worked on one of the four sides of the Mausoleum, and the fifth created the chariot on the roof. Around the base were sculptures of Greeks fighting Amazons, and further up were Greeks fighting Persians, together with hunting scenes; in between the columns of the

An artist's impression of the Mausoleum.

central section were rows of single human figures, possibly members of the Carian royal family; and lions, symbols of royalty, surrounded the edge of the roof. Two figures discovered during excavations in the nineteenth century almost certainly stood at the very top of the monument in the chariot and possibly represented Mausolus and Artemisia themselves.

It is interesting that the three main sections of the tomb were built in styles of architecture from three different cultures: the base is in the style of local Carian tombs; the middle section, or 'temple', is clearly Greek; while the roof looks like a stepped Egyptian pyramid. Perhaps Mausolus had a dream of uniting, in the new capital of his Carian kingdom, these different civilizations.

The tomb was still unfinished when Mausolus died in 353 BC, but his widow Queen Artemisia was determined to complete it as a symbol of her love. We are told that she spent all of Caria's wealth on it and made the kingdom bankrupt. But the sculptors were by then so devoted to their work that they finished it without pay. Another story tells us that Artemisia was so full of grief at her husband's death that she saved some of his ashes from his funeral and, mixing them with wine, drank some every day.

Artemisia was the sister of Mausolus as well as his wife. As in Egypt, it was a Carian custom for a king to marry his own sister. In fact, under Carian law a king's son could only inherit the throne if he followed this custom. But the relationship between Mausolus and Artemisia was clearly a very special one, and the magnificent tomb became a famous symbol of the love of wife and husband, like the Taj Mahal in India.

Artemisia's great sorrow did not, however, prevent her from being a strong ruler. When the Greeks of Rhodes heard that the Carian king was dead, they decided to attack Halicarnassus, thinking that a female ruler would offer little resistance. But the Carians under her leadership taught them a lesson. They tricked the Rhodians, captured their ships and used them to sail to Rhodes and attack the capital city.

Only two years after her husband's death, Artemisia died too. Her ashes probably joined his in the marble and gold urn that had been placed in a burial chamber dug out of solid rock beneath the Mausoleum, with steps leading down to it. There they remained undisturbed for over eighteen hundred years. The king and his queen would have been sad to see the changed fortunes of Caria during those centuries. The kingdom became part of the Roman empire for a time, but then the importance of the splendid city of Halicarnassus declined. The harbour, like that of Ephesus further north, became full of sand and mud, and the city was finally abandoned. Then, some time in the thirteenth century AD, an earthquake badly damaged the Mausoleum and turned it into ruins.

In the fifteenth century, Christian crusaders from Europe, called the Knights of St John, came from Rhodes to Asia Minor. In 1402 they began to build a huge castle, dedicated to Saint Peter, where the palace of Mausolus had once stood. Their plan was to use this as a base from which to attack Turkish territory in their fight against Islam. In 1494 they decided to strengthen their castle, and used the remains of the Mausoleum in order to do so. For twenty-eight years they removed stone after stone, sculpture after sculpture. They broke up many of the sculptures to use as building material, but they preserved some by building them into the castle walls.

When the Knights had cleared the ground of the ruins of the Mausoleum, they began to dig into the foundations for more stone. After a few days they discovered the entrance

Bodrum harbour and the Castle of St Peter.

into the underground burial chamber. In it was a beautiful
marble sarcophagus, in which the bones of Mausolus had
probably been placed. They also noticed the funeral urn
but, because night was approaching and they were afraid to
remain outside the castle for long, they left their discovery
unguarded. When they returned the next morning, the
coffin had been robbed and a few pieces of gold cloth and
decorations were all that remained.

Their great castle, despite their efforts to strengthen it,
did not protect the Knights of St John for long. The year
after they had discovered the burial chamber, the Knights
were attacked by the Turks and driven out of Asia Minor
and nearby Rhodes. So the unfortunate use they had made
of the remains of the Mausoleum had not achieved its
purpose. By a stroke of luck, however, the Knights had
failed to discover pieces of the chariot group from the top of
the tomb. Because of their position, these had fallen further

away than the rest of the building in the earthquake that brought them down and soon became covered with earth in a neighbouring field.

These sculptures were discovered by Charles Newton, a British archaeologist, during excavations which he carried out on the site of the Mausoleum in 1856–58. They include one of the horses of the chariot group, as well as the two statues already mentioned which may have represented King Mausolus and Queen Artemisia standing in the chariot. They are now in the British Museum. Further excavations were carried out by Danish archaeologists in 1966–77. One of their interesting finds, at the entrance to the burial chamber, was the remains of food which, it seems, had been buried with Mausolus so that he would not be hungry on his journey to the next world.

So what should we think of the effort to preserve the fame and glory of Mausolus with a magnificent tomb? The Greek writer Lucian, who was born about AD 120, asked himself the same question and gave his answer in his *Dialogues of the Dead*, which contain an imaginary conversation in the underworld between Mausolus and the Greek philosopher Diogenes:

'Tell me, Carian,' says Diogenes, 'why are you so proud and why do you expect to be honoured more than the rest of us?'

'Because,' replies Mausolus, 'I was handsome and tall and victorious in war. But most of all, because I have lying over me in Halicarnassus a gigantic monument such as no other dead person has, decorated in the finest way with statues of horses and men carved most realistically from the best quality marble.'

Diogenes answers: 'My handsome Mausolus, your strength and beauty are no longer with you here. If we were to have a beauty contest, I can't see why your skull should be thought better than mine. And as for your tomb and that expensive marble, it may give the people of Halicarnassus something to be proud of and to show to tourists, but I can't see what benefit you get from it, being weighed down by so much stone.'

'Is all this nothing, then?' asks Mausolus. 'Are Mausolus and Diogenes equal?'

'No, your highness,' replies Diogenes, 'we are not equal. Mausolus will groan when he remembers things on earth which he thought brought him happiness, while Diogenes will laugh at him. Mausolus will talk of the tomb built for him at Halicarnassus by his wife Artemisia, while Diogenes does not even know if his body has a tomb. Nor does he care. He has left to those who come after him an account of the life of a good man, an account that is more uplifting than your memorial, and built on surer foundations.'

Dates

BC

1000	Founding of Halicarnassus in Caria.
546	Caria becomes part of the Persian empire.
377	Mausolus becomes governor of Caria.
353	Death of Mausolus, while the Mausoleum is being built.
350	Death of Artemisia.

AD

655	Halicarnassus falls to the Arabs and is abandoned.
1402	Knights of St John build the Castle of St Peter.
1494–1522	Rebuilding of the castle.
1523	Knights abandon the castle to the Turks.
1856–58	First excavations of the site of the Mausoleum.
1966–77	Danish excavations.

Measurements

Total height of Mausoleum:	43 metres
Height of bottom section:	20 metres
Area of base:	Approximately 33 metres by 33 metres

The Colossus of Rhodes

The word *colossus* comes from a Greek word which was used at first for any large statue. Later, however, it came to be used especially for the huge statue that was built on the island of Rhodes at the beginning of the third century BC. (We normally say that a statue is made, not built, but we shall see that for the Colossus of Rhodes the second word is more suitable.) Today, in English, a *colossus* means a giant person; and the adjective *colossal* can refer to anything that is huge.

Rhodes is the name both of the Greek island in the Mediterranean off the coast of Turkey and of its capital city, which is at the north-eastern tip of the island. It was founded in 408 BC, when the inhabitants of the three main towns – Lindus, Ialysus and Camirus – decided to come together to create a capital for the whole island. They chose a place where the coast forms natural harbours, which they improved by building strong walls, or moles, into the sea. The city itself was planned and built in the form of a grid, that is to say, with straight streets crossing at right angles. Soon it had over 60,000 inhabitants, about twice the present number.

For a hundred years the city and the whole island enjoyed peace and prosperity. The Rhodians were great traders in the Mediterranean and had a large and active fleet of ships. In particular they traded with Egypt to the south. Egypt was part of the Persian empire until it fell to Alexander the Great in 332 BC and was included in his own huge empire. When Alexander died in 323, several of his generals fought each other in order to seize territory for themselves. One of these generals was Ptolemy, who marched into Egypt. The island of Rhodes became his ally.

Another of Alexander's generals, Antigonus, took over the south-western part of Anatolia before going on to make war on Ptolemy. He defeated Ptolemy's fleet off Cyprus in 306 BC and, now calling himself King Antigonus, decided to conquer Rhodes, Egypt's ally. The first thing to do was to take its capital city and to make use of its splendid harbours. For this purpose he sent to the island an army of 40,000 men, together with 30,000 workmen including engineers, all in a fleet of nearly four hundred ships under the command of his son Demetrius.

It was 305 BC, and Demetrius was thirty-four years old. He had won such fame for himself in the siege of cities that he was called Poliorcetes, or 'The Besieger'. At Rhodes, however, he first attacked the harbours, but without success. So he turned his attention to attacking from the land.

He ordered the building of a siege tower 45 metres high, much higher than the walls of the city. It had a frame of wood and iron covered with plates of metal. These protected the soldiers, who stood on wooden platforms and fired missiles from catapults and stone-throwers, through openings in the plates. The tower was fitted at the base with large, wide wheels so that it could be moved wherever it was needed. It was actually given a name: Helepolis, or 'Taker of Cities'.

But the tower did not live up to its name. The siege of Rhodes went on for a full year and, despite his own name of 'The Besieger', Demetrius was unsuccessful in taking the city. He made holes in its walls, but these were bravely defended and repaired by its citizens. In the end Demetrius gave up his attempt to conquer Rhodes and sailed away to fight in Greece, leaving all his siege engines behind him.

His father Antigonus was killed in battle a few years later, but Demetrius himself became king of Macedonia in 294 BC and ruled there for seven years.

Meanwhile the Rhodians made good use of his siege equipment. They sold it all for 300 talents, a talent being approximately 25 kilograms of silver. With this money, they decided to build something to express their thanks to their principal god for defending the city. The result was the Colossus of Rhodes, a statue of Helios, the god of the sun.

Helios was worshipped in many parts of the Greek world, but in particular on this island, which was given to him by Zeus. Every year the Rhodians made a sacrifice to Helios of a chariot and four horses, which they threw into the sea.

The Rhodians chose the sculptor Chares, who came from the island town of Lindus, to build this great statue. He was a pupil of Lysippus, who had been the favourite sculptor of Alexander the Great. But the statue that Chares now set about making was to be far bigger than anything that had been attempted before. Perhaps the idea for its great size came from Rhodes' ally Egypt, the home of several huge stone statues, including the famous Sphinx.

Chares started building his statue in 294 BC, ten years after Demetrius had sailed away from the island. It was finished about twelve years later. We do not know for certain what the statue looked like, because no clear descriptions or drawings of it made at the time have come down to us. But from what is known of other Greek statues of the period, and of the way this one was built, most experts think that it was the figure of man, probably naked, standing with his feet together and holding a torch above his head and a spear by his side. From its feet to the top of the torch the statue was 33 metres high.

Few statues have since been made which are larger

than the Colossus of Rhodes. Probably the best known is the Statue of Liberty, put up at the entrance to New York harbour in 1885. It is 46 metres high and, much like the Colossus, is made of copper sheets laid over a steel frame. Other very large statues include two war memorials, one being a statue of Mother Russia at Volgograd, formerly Stalingrad, and the other a figure of the Buddhist Goddess of Mercy near Tokyo. Both are over 45 metres high. The famous statue of Christ that overlooks the harbour at Rio de Janeiro is nearly 40 metres high.

We can be fairly certain about the height of the Colossus because several ancient writers give the same figure. These writers include Strabo, a Greek geographer born in 64 BC, and the Roman writer Pliny the Elder. Both were interested in fact rather than fiction, although neither could actually have seen the standing statue.

Another writer who gives the same figure for the statue's height is Philo of Byzantium. He was an engineer and his account is especially valuable because it tells us how the Colossus was built. Whereas most large statues, including the Statue of Liberty, were made in pieces which were then taken to the site and put together there, the Colossus was made where it stood. 'As when a house is built,' Philo says, 'the whole work had to rise upon itself.'

First of all the workers made a large base of white marble, on which the feet were then formed in bronze. The bronze was not solid but hollow, supported inside by an iron frame hammered to blocks of stone. Although Philo does not say so, the bronze was probably cast in the normal way in clay, that is to say, it was melted and poured into a clay mould, which was removed after the bronze had cooled.

The ankles were then cast in the same way on top of the feet. In order to work at the level they needed, Chares and his men covered what they had already made in a mound of

An artist's impression of the Colossus.

earth, so that the ground they stood on rose higher and higher like the statue itself. Since this was the way they worked, it is almost certain that the statue rose as close to a vertical line as possible, and that neither its arms nor any weapon such as a spear went out sideways.

The ankles, of course, had to be the strongest part of the whole statue, and for this reason alone they would have been placed close together and possibly supported at the back in some way. If, as it is thought, the statue was of a naked man, it did not have the advantage that was given to the Statue of Liberty of being clothed in a robe which comes right down to her feet – and therefore helps her to stand up!

In order to guess what the head looked like, we have to go to the Rhodian coins of the period. These show the head of a young man with quite long hair. We know that these heads represent the god Helios because some of them are surrounded by rays like those used around pictures of the sun. It is therefore quite possible that the head of Colossus was surrounded by bronze rays.

The idea that the statue held a torch was very strong in the Middle Ages. It was even believed then that the Colossus served as a lighthouse, but this is almost certainly not true. If a real torch did exist, how could anyone have got up to it to keep the fire alight? Unlike the Statue of Liberty, the Colossus certainly did not have stairs inside it or a look-out place in its head for tourists.

The amount of bronze used for the Colossus was, says Philo, huge, and was supplied by the copper and tin mines of 'the whole world'. He tells us that it cost the Rhodians 500 talents and that they also spent 300 talents on the iron used in the statue's framework. This, together with the stone centre, took more time and labour than did the outside of bronze.

Chares and his workmen did their work well. The statue stood, resisting the force of the winds, for fifty-six years and was only brought down by an earthquake. But where did it stand? This question, like the one about the statue's appearance, will perhaps never be answered with certainty. People in the Middle Ages and later, for whom the Colossus seems to have been the most interesting of the Seven Wonders, thought it stood at the entrance to one of the harbours of Rhodes, known now as the Madraki harbour. Moreover, they placed it with one foot on each side of the harbour entrance, so that ships could pass between its legs. Shakespeare himself seems to have had the same idea when he wrote the following lines in his play *Julius Caesar*:

> *Why, man, he doth bestride the narrow world*
> *Like a Colossus; and we petty men*
> *Walk under his huge legs ...*

The traditional view of the Colossus.

The world may have been 'narrow' for Shakespeare and for Julius Caesar, but the entrance to the Mandraki harbour measures at least 400 metres across, too wide for the Colossus, even supposing that it could have stood with its legs apart. Clearly this idea, however romantic, is one we must give up.

However, people have continued to suggest that the Colossus stood near the mouth of the Mandraki harbour, but on one side. They suggest that it stood on one of the moles, in the form that we have come to accept, that is, with its legs together rather than apart. This is possible: after all, there is a long tradition of placing statues at harbour mouths. There were several of them in the ancient world, and the Statue of Liberty is a modern example. The Colossus may have stood where the Fort St Nicholas now stands at the harbour entrance, and the old stone used in building the fort may have come from the giant statue.

But before we consider further the question of where the Colossus of Rhodes stood, we should first talk of its fall. This happened in 226 BC, in an earthquake that destroyed much of the city. One ancient writer says that in its fall the statue knocked down many houses. If this is true, it is unlikely that it stood at a harbour mouth, such as that of Mandraki, for then it would have probably fallen into the sea. And even if it had fallen onto the narrow mole itself, this is not the kind of place where there would have been many houses. With this kind of argument in mind, it has been suggested that the Colossus stood within the city itself.

The present city of Rhodes goes back to the Middle Ages but not beyond. It is built on top of the ancient city. Much of this has been excavated, and some archaeologists believe that they have discovered where the Temple of Helios stood. Since the Colossus was built in honour of the sun god Helios, it is suggested that the statue would have been built close to the temple. There is now an old Turkish school there, with a good deal of ancient stone at its base. So the question of where the Colossus stood should, perhaps, rest there until further excavations are carried out.

When the giant statue fell in the earthquake of 226 BC, it lay where it had fallen for nearly nine hundred years. Ptolemy III of Egypt, whose country was still a faithful ally of Rhodes, offered to pay to have it repaired. But the

Rhodians had been told by an oracle that they should leave the Colossus where it lay. It appears to have caused more interest lying on the ground than it had when it was standing up: people could now measure its huge size against their own bodies.

Pliny the Elder, who lived after the Colossus had fallen, wrote in his *Natural History*: 'Few people can make their arms meet round the thumb of the figure, and the fingers are larger than most statues; and where the limbs have broken off, enormous cavities yawn, while inside are seen great masses of rock with...which the artist steadied it when he erected it.' Strabo the geographer mentions the fallen statue too. He says that it broke off at the knees.

And so the Colossus lay, and people whom we might call the world's first tourists came to see it. Then in AD 654 the Arabs conquered the island of Rhodes together with its capital city. They cut the bronze of the Colossus into pieces and took them to the mainland, where they sold them to a merchant. It is said that he had to use nine hundred camels to carry them away.

Dates

BC

408	City of Rhodes founded.
305	Demetrius besieges Rhodes.
294–282	Building of the Colossus.
226	Colossus falls in an earthquake.

AD

654	Colossus is cut up, taken to the mainland and sold.
1885	Statue of Liberty erected at the entrance to New York Harbour.

Measurements

Height of Colossus:	33 metres
Height of Statue of Liberty:	46 metres

The Pharos at Alexandria

It is surprising to think that what was probably the first lighthouse in history was almost certainly the highest and probably the largest that the world has even seen. It was built in the third century BC and took its name of Pharos from the island on which it stood. And it stood there for over fifteen hundred years, and in working order for nearly a thousand, and so lasted longer than any of the other Seven Wonders except the Great Pyramid.

The island of Pharos was at the western edge of the mouth of the River Nile in Egypt, where Alexander the Great founded his city of Alexandria in 331 BC. As part of Alexander's plan for the city, the island was joined to the mainland by an artificial mole 1.2 kilometres long. In this way, two large harbours were formed, one on each side of the mole, protected from the open sea. Merchant ships used the western harbour, and warships used the eastern one. Through the years, land has been added on either side of the mole, and it has become a kilometre wide, so that we can no longer call Pharos an island.

Alexandria was planned from the beginning to be not only the proud capital of Egypt but also an important port. It became both of these things. With its wide, straight streets crossing at right angles, its royal palaces, its famous library, its museum of arts and sciences where scholars could live and study free of charge, and with Alexander the

Great's magnificent tomb and other monuments, it was perhaps the finest city of the Mediterranean world. It was without doubt its greatest port and centre of trade. This was because it could trade with both Europe and the East.

Immediately to the south of Alexandria lies Lake Marout, or Lake Mareotis as it was known in ancient times. This lake connects with the waterways of the mouth of the Nile. Alexander's engineers made a canal which ran from the merchant harbour into the lake. As a result, ships could pass between the port of Alexandria and the River Nile itself. Goods then travelled overland from the Nile to the Red Sea, and in this way trade was carried on with eastern countries as far away as India. In the other direction, that is to say westwards, goods from Alexandria are known to have reached the British Isles.

In its earliest days, however, Alexandria had a serious disadvantage as a centre of trade: sailors in the Mediterranean had difficulty in finding and entering the port. This was because the land at the mouth of the Nile is very flat, and so a sailor did not know where he was until he was near the coast and sometimes in danger of being blown onto it. Also, in this part of the Mediterranean, sand brought down by the Nile forms underwater banks which run parallel with the shore. Diodorus of Sicily, a Greek historian who lived in the first century BC, had this to say:

'A sandbank extends along nearly the whole length of Egypt, unseen to any who approach without previous experience of these waters. And so those sailors who think that they have escaped the danger of the sea, and in their ignorance turn with gladness towards the shore, suffer unexpected shipwreck.'

Clearly something had to be done to try and make the most important port in the Mediterranean a friendly place, easy to find and enter, on an unfriendly and sometimes dangerous coast. Fires, or burning beacons, were already used in the ancient world to guide ships to land; they are mentioned by the Greek poet Homer, who lived about five hundred years before the founding of Alexandria. But, on a coast as flat as that of Egypt, a sailor would not have seen these fires soon enough to be safely guided through the dangers that lay ahead. And so the idea for a giant tower with a fire on top – in other words a lighthouse – was born. The result was a remarkable building.

The lighthouse at Alexandria was probably begun in 297 BC, during the reign of King Ptolemy I, who ruled from 323 to 282 BC. He had been one of Alexander the Great's generals. When Alexander died in 323, his generals fought among themselves for pieces of his huge empire. Ptolemy, with part of the Macedonian army, seized Egypt. In this way he became the first of a line of rulers of Egypt that ended with the famous Cleopatra (68–30 BC). It was during the reign of his son Ptolemy II (282–246) that the Pharos was completed.

We do not know for certain who the architect was, but he was possibly a man called Sostratus of Cnidos, a town in Anatolia. His name appeared high up on the front of the lighthouse in large letters made of lead which were sunk into the wall. The name formed part of an inscription mentioned by later writers, including Pliny the Elder (AD 23–79). He says that Sostratus was the architect of the lighthouse. However, it was more usual in ancient times to inscribe on a building the name of the person who paid for it rather than the person who designed it, and Pliny may have been mistaken. Whatever part Sostratus had in the making of the Pharos – that is to say, whether he designed it or whether he paid for it – the inscription said that he intended it for the safety of 'those who sail the seas'.

Pliny goes on to say that the Pharos cost 800 talents to

build. (A talent was about 25 kilograms of silver.) In saying this he no doubt told the truth, as it must have been a very expensive building. But he tells us little more about the lighthouse, and we have to rely on other sources to know what it looked like and how large it was.

For a guide to its appearance we have a number of coins which were made and used in Alexandria during the first and second centuries AD, when Egypt was part of the Roman empire; on one side they proudly show the Pharos. There is also the written record of an Arab visitor to Alexandria over nine hundred years after it was built. This adds to what we know from the coins, and tells us something about its position and structure as well.

The Pharos stood at the eastern tip of the island from which it took its name. It did not stand on the island itself but on a very large stone platform built on top of rocks, and was connected with the island by a kind of stone bridge of sixteen arches. The platform was about 100 metres square and rose between seven and ten metres above the surface of the sea. Beneath it were rooms and, it seems, a huge tank for water.

The lighthouse itself was made of white marble. It consisted of three sections, built one on top of the other, of decreasing size. The first section was a large four-sided tower with many windows in its sides and a low wall, or parapet, at its top. Above this there was an eight-sided section about half the height of the bottom one. It also had windows and a parapet. Then, finally, there was a cylindrical section which was where the light of the Pharos came from. This was nearly a third of the height of the second section. It probably had a pointed, or conical, roof and was, at least in part, open to the air.

The coins made at Alexandria show us that there was a statue on top of the lighthouse. This was of a male figure holding a long stick-like object. The statue was almost certainly of Zeus, the father of the Greek gods, holding his thunderbolt, or of his brother the sea-god Poseidon, with his large 'fork' or trident. The coins also show us that at each corner of the huge bottom tower there was a statue of Triton blowing his horn. Triton was half man, half fish, the son of Poseidon by his wife Amphitrite, goddess of the sea and, in particular, of the Mediterranean. This suggests that the statue at the top was of Poseidon. On the other hand, Zeus was sometimes given the title of Soter, or 'he who saves', a title used by Ptolemy I himself. So the builders of the lighthouse may have wished, by putting up a statue of Zeus, to honour their king.

In AD 1166, that is to say nearly fifteen hundred years after it was built and five hundred years after the Muslim conquest of Alexandria, the Pharos was still standing, although, as we shall see, it had changed slightly in appearance. A visitor to the lighthouse in that year, Yusuf Ibn al-Sheik, has left us a detailed account of what he saw. He took measurements using a piece of string – clearly a very long one – with a stone tied to the end, and we can judge that these were fairly accurate. He begins by describing the platform, together with its rooms, on which the lighthouse was built, and the stone bridge that we have already mentioned. He then enters the lighthouse itself.

He says that inside there were no stairs but a wide stone pathway, or ramp, going round and round a large central stone column in a spiral, leading upwards to the top of the first section of the lighthouse. When he got there he let down his string; it measured 57.7 metres. Inside the octagonal second section there were stairs. When he had climbed these he found that he was 27.45 metres above the top of the first section. The third section was 7.32 metres high. Above it, instead of the statue shown on the

Alexandrian coins, there was now a mosque with a domed roof. Yusuf says that this was 5.49 metres high (although here one wonders how he was able to measure it).

An artist's impression of the Pharos.

If we say that the original conical roof of the Pharos and its statue were, taken together, approximately the same height as the mosque which replaced them, and if we add the height above sea level of the platform on which the lighthouse stood, then we get a figure for the total height of the Pharos of 105–108 metres. This is greater than the height of any stone lighthouse that has since been built. The great lighthouse of Ushant off the western coast of France is 100 metres high. There is a light at the top of a 106-metre high steel structure off the port of Yokohama in Japan, but that is not a lighthouse in the true sense of the word, for it is not a 'house', or roofed building.

As for the question of how the lighthouse produced its light, the ancient writers tell us nothing to help us; nor does Yusuf writing in the early Middle Ages. The Jewish historian Josephus, who lived in the first century AD, says that sailors could see the light at night from 60 kilometres away. In that case, the Pharos was able not only to produce a very strong light but also to direct it in a certain direction. So we must ask ourselves first what it was that the keepers of the Pharos burnt as fuel and, secondly, how they sent out the light they produced.

Wood was burnt for the production of light in lighthouses as recently as the last century. We might therefore think that this gives us our answer straight away. The spiral ramp mentioned by Yusuf suggest that animals such as donkeys were used to carry fuel to the top of the first section of the lighthouse. If the fuel was wood, a great deal would have been needed. The problem is that there was then, just as now, very little wood in Egypt. There were no forests. It would have been necessary to bring in the wood from abroad.

There are, however, at least two other possibilities. One is that the fuel might have been animal dung. This is still burnt in countries where wood is scarce. Alternatively, it might have been mineral oil, that is to say, petroleum, which Greeks at that time had already discovered. Whatever the fuel, it was almost certainly burnt in the second, or octagonal, section of the lighthouse.

And so we come to the question of how the keepers of the Pharos caught the light from the fire and sent it out across the sea. It is generally agreed that this was done with large sheets of polished brass placed inside the top cylindrical section. In the daytime these reflectors may have been used to catch and reflect the rays of the sun. On dull, sunless days the Pharos itself, a giant pillar of white marble, would have been visible to sailors and served as their guide as they approached the most famous port of the ancient Mediterranean world.

Although, as we have seen, the Pharos was still standing in AD 1166, when it was visited by Yusuf Ibn al-Sheik, it is very doubtful that it was still being used as a lighthouse by then; Yusuf describes it as if it were abandoned and already an ancient monument. Alexandria had ceased to be the capital of Egypt in AD 641 when its Arab conquerors founded a new capital where Cairo now stands; and it had lost much of its importance as a Mediterranean port. The need for a working lighthouse was no longer as great as it had been.

However, the Pharos continued to stand for nearly another 140 years after AD 1166. It had survived earthquakes in the years 690 and 956, and it continued to be a witness to the skills of its architect and builders. Then finally, in 1303, an earthquake damaged it badly, and another one in 1323 caused more damage. The writer Ibn Battuta who visited the ruins in 1349 says that fallen stones prevented him from reaching what was left of the bottom section, or main tower. In the following century the ruins were cleared away and in their place – and built with the stones of the Pharos – rose the fort of Qait Bey, which still stands today.

Meanwhile, however, the Pharos had had its children. Following the example it had set, the Romans had built about forty lighthouses in and around the Mediterranean world, although none was as large as its parent. Several of them are still standing. There is one in England and one in France, on each side of the English Channel.

The one in England, at the town of Dover, is known to this day as the Pharos. This is also the modern Greek name for a lighthouse. Forms of the name occur in several other languages, meaning not only a lighthouse but also a car headlight: *phare* in French, *faro* in Italian, Portuguese and Spanish, and *far* in Albanian. And so the Pharos of Alexandria, like the Mausoleum at Halicarnassus and the Colossus of Rhodes, is still with us in the use we make of its name.

Dates

BC

331	Founding of the city of Alexandria.
297–280	Building of the Pharos.

AD

641	Arab conquest of Egypt.
1166	Pharos described by Yusuf Ibn al-Sheik.
1303 & 1323	Pharos badly damaged in earthquakes.
1349	Ibn Battuta visits the ruins.
1480	Qait Bey fort built on the site of the Pharos.

Measurements

Height of lower section:	57.7 metres
Height of middle section:	27.45 metres
Height of upper section:	7.32 metres
Total height of Pharos (with base and statue):	105–108 metres
Area of base:	Approximately 100 metres by 100 metres

Glossary

The meanings given are those which the words have in the text.

abandon	to leave completely alone
ally	a state or country which helps you in a war
altar	a special table used for religious purposes
amphitheatre	a large open theatre with rows of raised seats around it
astrology	predicting the future by studying the stars and planets
astronomy	the study of the stars and planets
bankrupt	owing more money than you can pay
beacon	a fire made on high ground as a signal
beam	a thick horizontal bar that helps to support the weight of a building
bestride	to stand with one leg on each side of
bitumen	a black sticky substance
brass	a bright yellow metal
bronze	a dark yellowish-brown metal
bull	the male of the cow
burial	the act of putting a dead body in its grave
camel	a kind of animal often used for transport in the desert
capture	to take as a prisoner
carving	a picture cut into wood or stone
catapult	a machine for firing very heavy arrows
cavity	a hollow space in something solid
cease	to stop
chamber	a room used for a special purpose
charcoal	a black substance made by burning wood very slowly
chariot	a small cart with two wheels, pulled by horses
coffin	a box for a dead body
conical	in the shape of a cone, having a round base and sides that come to a point at the top
conquest	conquering another place and its people

courtyard	an open walled space inside a large building
craftsman	a skilled worker who makes things by hand
crusader	in the **Middle Ages**, a Christian fighter in the wars against Islam
cylindrical	in the shape of a cylinder, having a round base and straight sides
decline	to go down in importance
dedicate	to declare that something is in honour of a certain person
deserted	empty, without people
devoted to	loving something very much
domed	having a rounded roof
dung	animal waste
embalm	to treat a dead body with oils and spices to keep it whole
excavate	to dig up carefully
execute	to kill someone who has been found guilty of a crime
flee	(past tense *fled*) to run away because you are afraid
fleet	a group of ships under one commander
footstool	a low piece of furniture used to rest your feet on
fort	a special **fortified** building to defend an area
fortified	protected with strong walls etc.
found	to start building (a town or city)
foundations	the solid base of building, deep in the ground
gallery	a high platform along the inside walls of a building
granite	a kind of hard, grey rock
grief	great sorrow at someone's death
groan	to make a deep cry of pain
harbour	a safe place for ships
hive	the place where bees live
homesick	unhappy because you are away from home
horn	a simple musical instrument that you blow into
hospitality	welcoming guests or strangers
huntress	a female hunter
inhabitants	the people who live in a place
inherit	to become the owner of something when another person dies
inscription	words written on something as a lasting record
invade	to attack another country by entering it with your army
ivory	hard white bone from an elephant's tusks
knight	a noble man trained to fight on horseback

lead	a very heavy metal
lever	a bar pushed under a heavy object to lift it
lighthouse	a tall building on the coast that sends out light to guide ships
limestone	a kind of white rock
magnificent	important-looking, impressive
marble	a kind of hard stone which is polished and used for building
massive	extremely big
memorial	something built or done in memory of a person or event
meteorite	a small piece of rock or metal that has fallen to the earth from space
Middle Ages	the period of history between about AD 1100 and 1500
missile	an object or weapon thrown or fired at an enemy
mole	a thick wall built in the sea
monument	a building in memory of a person or event
mould	a hard container in the shape of an object being made, into which soft material is poured
mound	a small man-made hill
mummy	an **embalmed** body
mythology	stories from the past about supernatural events
octagonal	eight-sided
oracle	a religious place where people ask questions about the future
pagan	non-Christian (nowadays: not belonging to any of the major religions)
pentathlon	an athletic event in which people compete in five different sports
petty	small and unimportant
plain	an area of flat land
plank	a long flat piece of wood
post	a piece of wood which stands up to support something
precious	very valuable
prosperity	success and wealth
proverb	a well-known wise saying
pulley	lifting equipment consisting of a wheel and a rope which moves over it
ramp	a man-made slope connecting two levels
ray	a beam of light
reed	a tall plant that grows in wet places
remains	all that remains of something
robe	a long garment or dress
roller	a hard object shaped like a tube that rolls over and over

ruins, in	destroyed, with only a few walls and stones left
sacred	connected with religion
sacrifice	to kill as part of a religious ceremony
sarcophagus	a stone box for a dead body
sceptre	a rod carried by a king etc. as a symbol of power
sculptor	an artist who makes **sculptures**
sculpture	a work of art made by cutting wood, stone etc.
seek	(past tense *sought*) to look for
seize	to take hold of suddenly
shipwreck	the destruction of a ship which hits something or sinks
shrine	a holy place, special to one person or god
siege	a long attack on a city
silversmith	a person who makes things of silver
site	the exact place where something was
skull	the bone of a head
spear	a long weapon with a pointed end which you throw at an enemy
spiral	a curve that winds round and round
statue	a large figure of a person, usually made of wood, stone or metal
structure	a building
survive	to live through something dangerous
temple	a building used for the worship of a god
terraces	a series of raised level areas
thereby	in that way
throne	the chair of a king or queen (or the power which it represents)
thunderbolt	a crash of thunder with a flash of lightning
tomb	a place where a dead person is buried, usually made of stone
torch	a burning piece of wood used as a light
tragic	causing great sadness
trident	a large fork with three points
truce	an agreement to stop fighting for a certain period of time
twin	one of two children born at the same time of the same mother
urn	a container for the ashes of a dead person
workshop	a room used for making or repairing things in
worship	to show great respect to, as to a god
wrestling	a form of fighting in which you try to throw the other person to the ground